T0128772

Critical Acclaim for Bunkai!

by Taniguchi Takao, 5th dan JKA
Terai-machi, Ishikawa-ken, Japan

The Tekki kata have been with karate-ka for many years, even much before the creation and formalization of the Japan Karate Association. These kata have been fundamental kata and required knowledge for the serious karate enthusiast. Dr. Schmeisser has done something with these kata which has, to date, not been done well by any karate instructors both in Japan and overseas.

Whether or not many instructors were unsure of what the techniques in the Tekki kata meant, or if they were never properly instructed themselves, is not sure. This text, *Bunkai: Secrets of Karate Kata: Volume 1,* is one which is carefully organized and pays a high degree of attention to each technique as one flows to the next. Although many instructors have different interpretations of the Tekki kata, this book is coherent, easy to understand, and firmly rooted in a sense of reality. Dr. Schmeisser has done what many instructors have not yet been able to demonstrate, a cohesive and articulate interpretation of the techniques of the Tekki kata. This book is excellent not only for students, but for instructors of karate as well.

Kata without explanations and applications have no meaning. This book helps illuminate some of the less clear areas of these kata and does so with easy to follow illustrations. For kata to be meaningful it is critical for the practitioner to understand that every single movement has meaning. Dr. Schmeisser's interpretations are very accurate and sensible. Although English is not my first language, I can see very clearly what Dr. Schmeisser is doing through the text. It is a wonderful study for people interested in kata applications.

It is my sincere hope that such excellent work in kata explanation will continue. I wish Dr. Schmeisser all the best as he continues with his work in kata and in his helping future karate teachers understand more deeply our study in karate.

More Critical Acclaim!

by Tony Annesi, Takeshin Sogo Budo

author of *Cracking the Kata Code, The Road to Mastery,* and
The Principles of Advanced Budo

In the 1970's, karate-ka like myself longed for any little tidbit of information regarding kata application that was not blatantly overt. In fact, I took it upon myself to propose to a major martial arts publisher a volume called *Hidden Throws and Locks of Karate-do*. It was rejected because "many other books had been written on the subject." I guess the editors were not martial artists and did not understand that overt applications were not the more subtle or hidden meanings that many of my fellow martial artists and I were after.

Now I am overjoyed to see a similar, even more concentrated, volume brought to life by Dr. Elmar Schmeisser in his book *Bunkai: Secrets of Karate Kata*. In this compact book, Dr. Schmeisser opens the doors to *tegumi* (Okinawan grappling) as it is manifested in the popular Shotokan versions of the Iron Horseman forms. With no wasted space on preliminaries or filler, Dr. Schmeisser dives into the subject offering unique, imaginative, but nonetheless applicable, interpretations of karate forms which most practitioners have heretofore justified with fanciful and non-functional explanations. There is no excuse for that now.

Dr. Schmeisser is one of a few senior karate-ka who are investigating not just the kata itself, but the self-defense that comes from it—the reason the kata were created in the first place.

BUNKAI:
Secrets of Karate Kata

THE TEKKI SERIES

By
Elmar T. Schmeisser, Ph.D.
Kyoshi Nanadan (Shotokan), International Society
of Okinawan - Japanese Karate-Do
Master Instructor, American Teachers Association of the Martial Arts

*Neither the author nor the publisher accepts or assumes any responsibility
or liability for any personal injuries sustained by anyone as a result of
the use or practice of any of the instructions contained in this volume.*

Order this book online at www.trafford.com
or email orders@trafford.com

Most Trafford titles are also available at major online book retailers.

© Copyright 2019 Elmar T. Schmeisser, Ph.D.
All rights reserved. No part of this publication may be reproduced, stored in a retrieval
system, or transmitted, in any form or by any means, electronic, mechanical, photocopying,
recording, or otherwise, without the written prior permission of the author.

Print information available on the last page.

ISBN: 978-1-4907-9307-8 (sc)
ISBN: 978-1-4907-9309-2 (e)

Because of the dynamic nature of the Internet, any web addresses or links contained in
this book may have changed since publication and may no longer be valid. The views
expressed in this work are solely those of the author and do not necessarily reflect the
views of the publisher, and the publisher hereby disclaims any responsibility for them.

Any people depicted in stock imagery provided by Getty Images are models,
and such images are being used for illustrative purposes only.
Certain stock imagery © Getty Images.

Trafford rev. 01/24/2019

 www.trafford.com

North America & international
toll-free: 1 888 232 4444 (USA & Canada)
fax: 812 355 4082

DEDICATION

To my Colleagues in Karate:

The Way is not static and dead;
Learn from the old Masters,
Do not worship them;
Learn from your Teachers,
Do not blindly follow them;
Learn from your Students,
Do not assume you know all the Truth.

ACKNOWLEDGMENTS

Two of my senior students, Pete Knox and Noel Brewer, helped me (relatively uncomplainingly) to develop and refine these *bunkai*. Byron Edmonds and Mike Neeman posed for the photos as the attackers. Lorinda Lykins took the digital photographs.

Thanks are due to all, and to the many more across the years who have helped me evolve my understanding of karate

TABLE OF CONTENTS

PREFACE

I owe a strong debt of gratitude to the various teachers of the martial arts who did not ask about style or federation or affiliation or money or membership, but were truly interested in exploring the nature and variations of these arts as they have been passed down through history. To these people, and to others who believe that there is no absolute right or wrong in technique, but only variations of greater or lesser effectiveness depending on circumstance, I must say thanks. Context should always dictate technique, and no individual style or method can, by itself, be called complete, perfect, or supreme. It has been said before, but it bears repeating: There are no superior martial arts; there are only the people who make them so.

In the 16 years since "Bunkai: Secrets of Karate Kata Volume 1: The Tekki Series" was first published by Tamashii Press (2000), the karate world has undergone a renaissance in its practice of kata, at least in some sectors and with some instructors. Vince Morris, Ian Abernathy, Patrick McCarthy, Rick Clark and many others have taken the idea of self-defense applications to the heart of their practice of kata, and in Patrick McCarthy's case, in fact pioneered much of the field. In some styles, applications have always been taught to some extent with the kata, but in the Shotokan world, and the Japan Karate Association in particular, such was never the focus of kata. This book was originally intended to be a bridge for those coming from similar backgrounds, keeping them grounded in the performance of the kata as they knew them, and introducing relatively straight-forward application possibilities that could be extracted from the trajectories of the kata movements, based only on my personal study of the aikido and judo technical intersections with the karate kata movements. As such, even though the material is now dated and in excellent company, I believe this book can still fulfill that function for those individuals who desire to expand their practice of kata from a system of improving kihon, tai-sabaki, kime, etc. into an encyclopedia of combinations that can be practiced as one-step kumite against common street attacks. Working against classical karate-style stepping punch attack is again a useful bridge, but it should not stop there, if the kata, and by extension karate itself, is to be useful in possible street confrontations rather than being limited to tournament dueling between highly skilled karate-ka. Therefore I am republishing this material, somewhat updated to reflect the passage of time, as a resource for those interested in applications, but unwilling to completely abandon their many years of fulfilling practice.

INTRODUCTION

The *kata* series Tekki Shodan, Tekki Nidan and Tekki Sandan are standard *kata* in the JKA derived Shotokan curriculum of *kata*. They actually have older forms, called Naihanchi or Naifanshi, which differ in some details of hand position as well as in stance, but in general parallel the Tekki format quite closely. Tekki Shodan is commonly assigned to senior green belts (4th kyu — about a 2— to 3—year student) who has passed all five Heian *kata* and who are testing for brown belt (3rd kyu). Tekki Nidan and Tekki Sandan are usually reserved until after the attainment of Nidan (2nd degree black belt) in most JKA—style schools, although these *kata* profitably can be taught much earlier. Indeed, some schools of Okinawan karate start their curriculum with the 3 Tekki (Naifanchi) *kata* rather than with the five Heian (Pinan) *kata*.

The technique interpretations (*bunkai*) given below are only one of many possible methods of analysis. Previous *bunkai* for these *kata* have been published that use a selected subset of the movements. Occasionally, individual movements have been explained as having no immediate or practical use, or as being "set up" or "training" movements. Also, it has been claimed that many finishing movements, i.e.,movements that would complete a counterattack in the *kata* are only implied but actually have been left out of the *kata* itself. I disagree with both of these positions. As I see it, there are no movements that can be considered purely as a setup, i.e., do no damage to the opponent, nor are the *kata* movements incomplete, although their stylistic evolution may have blurred critical details. On the other hand, I believe the *kata* can be over—interpreted. One set of *bunkai* I have seen executes the entire *kata* on a single opponent as a very complex jujitsu—style coordination exercise.[1] I prefer a simpler, more directly self—defense oriented interpretation.

An item that may help to explain the *kata* techniques is actually an historical insight. These *kata* were developed before the modern arts now called "jujitsu," "karate," and "kobudo" were split into separate practices with separate lineages of instructors and independent curricula. Therefore, it would be logical to assume that these *kata* incorporate all these arts into their movements — it's all just self—defense. The reader will see that there are many movements portrayed here that are similar to movements in modern judo, aikido, jujitsu and bojitsu as well as common street wrestling in addition to the normally expected blocking, kicking and punching techniques of orthodox karate.

A further insight is that *kata* were developed as teaching tools as well as learning tools. As such, the *kata* must fulfill requirements for the teacher as well as for the student. Accordingly, the formal performance of the *kata* without an opponent may separate some movements actually used simultaneously, or may change the angle of movement so that the teacher can see the student(s) more clearly. For example, there are several twist stances (*kosa—dachi*) – these can imply a twist or turn in place rather than a linear step over. Movements may be done slowly in the *kata* because they are difficult and must be done correctly in learning them, even though many of them would be done at full speed in application. Movements may be repeated in *kata* because they were felt to be important, and needed special practice, not that their actual usage required repeated application of the same combination on the same implied attacker.

Within the constraints noted above, I have attempted to provide the student with a single continuous, consistent visualization for each movement in these *kata*, leaving no movement out and needing no overlap of one dynamic sequence into another. In this manner, the student can practice the *kata* in a mindful manner, not as calisthenics or as an archaic way to string strange basic techniques together, but as a way to develop and practice self—defense combinations. This is, of course, not the only set of techniques that could be visualized as arising from the movements in each *kata*. It should be noted that each technique or small series of techniques can be taken out of any *kata* and studied in isolation for possible alternate applications in self—defense.[2] They can be rearranged and recombined in any order.[3] This form of "posture analysis" can allow for a very wide range of meanings to be attached to any particular position in the *kata*. Posture analysis views *kata* as composed of independent applications with no more than two moves, at most three. By contrast, this book demonstrates "sequence analysis," and attempts to reduce the number of opponents dealt with in the entire *kata* to as few as possible. In both forms of analysis, every position of every limb must be accounted for in a manner that makes combat sense. However, it is obvious that with posture analysis, one can create and "bolt on" innumerable *bunkai*. As Tony Anessi says: "A block is a lock is a blow is a throw."[iii] With such a rich palette of meaning, it gets difficult (in my view) to assign unambiguous meanings to the movements of a *kata*. The longer a sequence of moves gets, the more restricted the universe of *bunkai* gets, until one is left with one or two *bunkai*, at most, that allow the whole sequence to make sense as a sequence. This is the approach I have taken, in the belief that the originator of the *kata* probably had only one *bunkai* in mind during its construction. The strength and value of *kata* training is that it is inclusive of these other interpretations, i.e., these other applications are not "wrong" in any sense of the word. The more uses a student can obtain from a movement or set of movements, the richer that student's experience of the *kata* will be, and the more useful the practice of the *kata* will be to their skill development.

The process of learning and then understanding any *kata* proceeds in several clearly definable steps. First, one learns the physical sequence by means of labels taken from the basic techniques: "punch," "inside block," and so on. After the sequence has been learned, a first level of *bunkai* can be explored by fitting opponents into these labeled techniques. At this level, a technique called a "block" is used to actually block an appropriate attack, and the attacker adjusts each motion to permit the "defense" defined by the formal *kata* shape to succeed. In general, a new opponent will be needed every two to three movements. It is at this point (or even before) that many schools stop their analysis of the *kata* in favor of either accumulating other *kata*, concentrating on basic technique, or practicing tournament sparring. However, after this preliminary level of *bunkai* has been practiced to the point that each technique can actually do its apparent job, a second level of *bunkai* analysis can begin.

At the second level of analysis, the labels for the individual techniques are discarded, and the movements themselves are explored for alternative uses as to their effects. Punches can become throws, blocks can become strikes or joint locking techniques, and steps can become kicks or stamping attacks. With more experience, the student attempts to fit opponents into the movements in as many different ways as possible, modifying the movements as little as possible in order to explore their principles.

Finally, moving the consideration from single movements to the combinations or short sequences shown in the *kata* can extend the analysis dramatically at this level. During this form of analysis, the student attempts to reduce the number of opponents implied by the *kata* to a minimum. As noted above, it is this level of analysis that I have attempted to show in this volume.

In all these analyses, there are a few basic principles that should be followed: (1) Each movement must do something useful (from the defender's point of view) to the opponent; (2) no opponent must be left in a condition to continue or resume an attack; and, (3) there must be a safety margin in case of the failure of any technique to achieve full effect.

Beyond the techniques shown here, the techniques in *kata* also can act simply as the springboard for further techniques not found in the particular *kata* under study. This amplification of the *kata* is often termed *oyo* or *bunkai—oyo*. In this type of training, a *kata* motion or set of motions is used to start a defense sequence, but the sequence is finished with other techniques not in that *kata* sequence. These other techniques can be taken from other portions of the same or different *kata*, or from techniques found in basic karate training.

Lastly, one can proceed to *henka—waza* (variation or varied techniques). These variations may have only a distant relationship to the *kata*, but arise from its principles or technical themes and show techniques that have been freely modified to produce the desired results. Too often, these latter types of analyses have been used to explain away *kata* motions for which the *bunkai* are not known or understood. This tendency is to be avoided, and both *oyo* and *henka* should be approached only after a reasonable set of direct *bunkai* are mastered.

Finally, there is a level of *bunkai* beyond the level presented here that is complementary rather than exclusive — that of *kyusho—jitsu*, or essentially "combat acupuncture." The techniques as presented here can be practiced (gently) with partners, since they include primarily jujitsu methods (or Okinawan *tuite* [grappling]) as well as the classical striking and kicking techniques of karate. *Kyusho—jitsu*, just as medical acupuncture, cannot be safely learned or practiced in any other venue than as a personal apprentice to a certified expert who has been trained to reverse the effects of any particular strike or combination of strikes. Therefore, *kyusho—jitsu* from the traditional Asian medicine viewpoint will not be explicitly addressed in this series. I have included targeting information in Western anatomical terms where appropriate, however.

The following sections are organized in parallel streams of image: The *kata* steps as performed solo by an individual, and the accompanying application as performed with a partner and captioned with appropriate descriptions.

TEKKI SHODAN

This *kata*, as indicated by its name, is the first of the three Tekki *kata*. The *kata* is performed on a single horizontal line (sideways). This *kata* is composed of two mirror imaged parts (rightwards and leftwards) to emphasize that these techniques need to be learned without preference as to which hand is to be used. Each part is itself composed (for this visualization) of two halves, each dealing with a single opponent. The transition between the mirror image halves is relatively obvious; the transition from the first to the second opponent occurs just before the cross step following the hook punch. For this performance of the *kata*, the breath alternates in and out with each technique.

 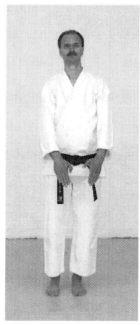 

1. The initial attack is a right leg front kick, which the *kata* answers by combining the first two movements: the *yoi* and the twist stance thus turning in place. This movement attacks a nerve on the inside of the shin, one palm width up from the ankle, and is performed on the in breath. The covering hand traps the leg for the following techniques.

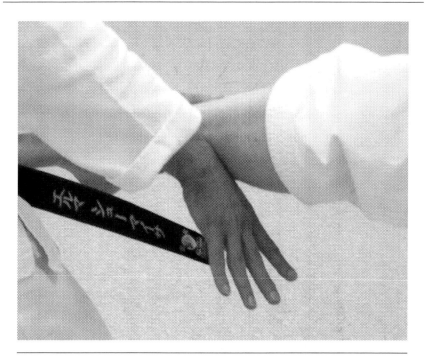

2. The follow up is a knee or shin kick into the bottom of the leg or the groin and a knife hand which rolls into a ridge hand strike to the carotid baroreceptor in the neck. During this, hold on to the leg to prevent the opponent's escape, and if possible stamp into the

opponent's stance leg. In the Shudokan style version of this *kata*, this leg movement, and all like it further in the *kata*, are performed as *nami—gaeshi* (returning wave kick), implying a strike with the foot targeted at the lower thigh, rather than with the shin or knee and a higher target.

3. Continuing with the same opponent, the combination proceeds in case the previous techniques did not complete the defense. Specifically, the leg is dropped to free up an elbow strike to the side of the face (under the ear or into the jaw hinge area) while the hand that initially struck the opponent's neck skips over the head to trap it, producing a hammer and anvil effect. The in breath is used for speed.

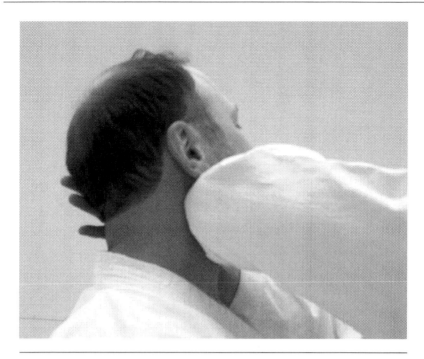

4. The "setup" movement results in taking the opponent's head and smashing the face into the crest of the hip bone, the motion focused with an out breath.

5. The "down block" occurs with the hair or collar captured in the "blocking" hand, so as to lever open the opponent's throat up for the next technique. Pressure with the "blocking" elbow into the back ensures that the opponent will bend their knees and drop their center. The hand left behind might have been holding onto the opponent's ear, or have been used to place pressure behind the jaw hinge or a thumb into the eye to encourage movement.

6. The sequence concludes with a short hook punch into the exposed throat (either the windpipe or the other carotid artery) as the holding hand prevents the head from escaping.

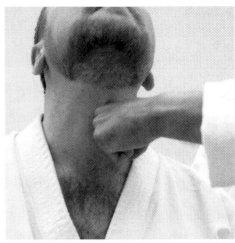

7.   The next technique signals a new opponent by stepping across. This *bunkai* assumes a right hand stepping punch. The movement escapes from the remaining threat hand, parries, and grabs with the pullback hand. The "blocking" hand attacks the elbow and at the very least locks it straight, unbalancing the attacker. During the step across is an in breath kick, and the technique completes on the out breath. Alternately, the cross step can be considered as the same indicator as the cross step in the beginning, i.e., a marker for a twist of 90 degrees to slip the incoming punch with the hand parry (thumb up).

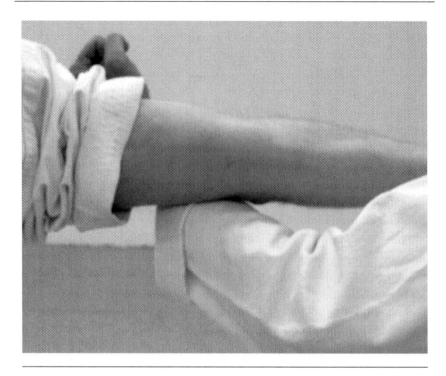

8. The next technique "clears" the opponent's attacking arm, lifting it up to expose the armpit or upper lateral ribcage area to a punch during the in breath.

9. The punching hand then grabs the shoulder, pulling it down while the previously "blocking" hand strikes in a rising manner into the neck upwards toward the jaw hinge area.

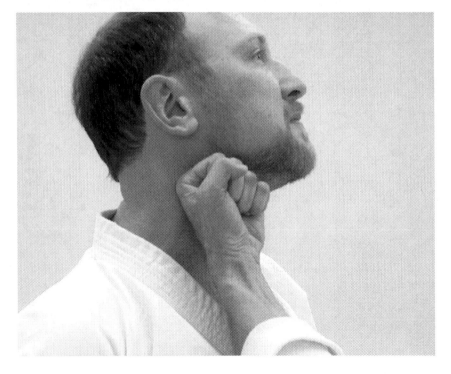

10. For the next techniques, the gripping hand does not release the opponent. The returning wave kick attacks the back of the leg, making the opponent lean back, buckling the knee, and exposing the throat to a subsequent hammer fist attack, breathing first in on the kick and then out on the strike.

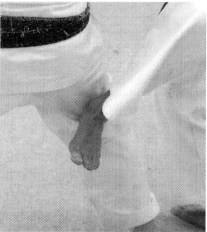

11. The next kick into the groin opens the back of the neck for a strike into the vertebral arteries giving shock directly to the brain stem.

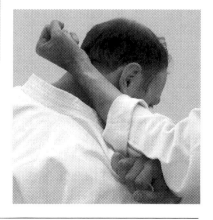

12. The combination returns to a face smash into the defender's hip, this time with an in breath.

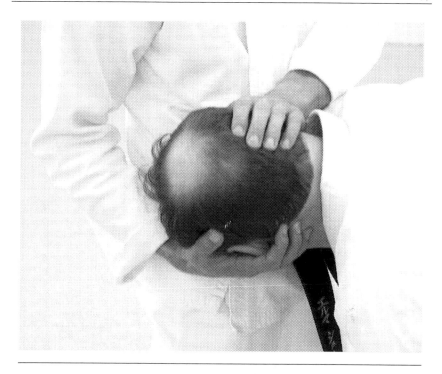

13. The *kata* sequence completes with a head twist, that can either act as a throw or as a neck break to finish the defense *<kiai>*.

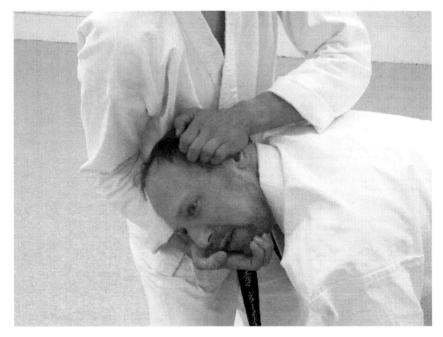

14. From here, the *kata* repeats in mirror image, starting with the leg strike and trap, breathing in. An alternative attack might be a grab of the defender's outstretched arm; the sweep would act to free the arm, take off the attacking hand, and then striking as before.

15. Neck strike (out breath). Alternatively, with a right handed grabbing attack, the sweeping arm might act as a throw.

16. Elbow strike to head (in breath)

17. Face smash (out breath). An alternative *bunkai* might include the concept of a new attacker at this point. The left hand might have grabbed an attacker's fist while the right hand on top delivers a back knuckle strike onto the back of that fist.

18. Opening "down block" movement (in breath). In the case of a close range attack in a second opponent scenario, the block might even be a block, but could also be a hammer fist strike on the way to the following hook punch.

19. Throat punch (out breath). A different interpretation might combine the motions of the down block and the hook punch to create a form of throw, with the down block inside the opponent's trapped left elbow and the hook punch pushing the fist over towards the opponent's face and then past their inside shoulder.

20. New opponent: cross step, parry, and kick (in breath) and elbow break (out breath).

21. Clear the target by lifting the arm and punching into the armpit (in breath).

22. Grab the shoulder, pull and strike into the neck (out breath).

23. Attack the back of the leg (in breath), hammer strike the throat (out breath).

24. Kick the groin (in breath), hammer strike the neck (out breath).

25. Repeat the face smash (again with an in breath).

26. Neck break or throw <out breath: *kiai*>.

27. This ends the *kata* <yame>.

TEKKI NIDAN

This *kata* is the second of the Tekki series. The lessons in this *kata* build on those of Tekki Shodan, using some of the same techniques, but incorporating them in different combinations. In this *kata*, many of the techniques are designed (for these *bunkai*) as methods to incapacitate an attacking arm. As in Tekki Shodan, the *kata* has four segments. However, while in Tekki Shodan these mirror parts are sequential halves, in Tekki Nidan, each segment's mirror image piece is done first, before the second half of the *kata* is started. This results in two very different feelings for the two halves of the *kata*: The first half is very smooth and flowing — almost like the internal Chinese martial arts, while the second half is very sharply focused, syncopated, and impact oriented. Again, there are four opponents in the entire *kata*, or (by ignoring the mirror halves) only two — one for the smooth portion and one for the more focused portion. The breathing is very rhythmical: The odd numbered counts are done breathing in, and even numbered counts are done breathing out.

1. The attack is a two—handed grab attempt from the rear. The attacker's left hand is taken off the shoulder with the right hand on the in breath, and the defender's left elbow is used to attack into the rib cage as the body sinks and turns counterclockwise 90 degrees.

2. The counter continues, turning towards the opponent with a front kick followed by a double strike into the biceps to weaken the arms. During this movement, there is a double inverted punch to the infraorbital ridges below the eyes (stepped out breath).

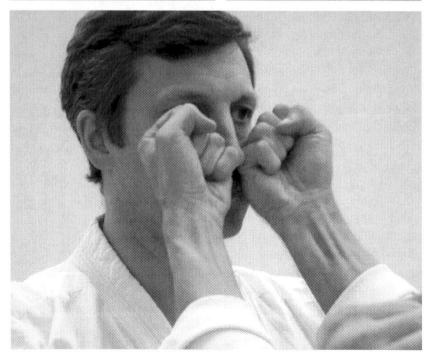

3. Moving away from the free arm by turning even farther, the initially captured arm is again trapped and the elbow hyperextended, stretching the opponent (breathe in for smoothness).

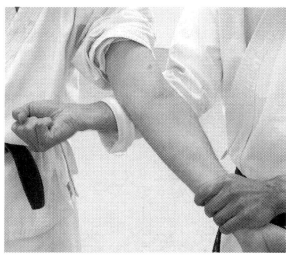

4. The sequence concludes with an entering movement into the opponent's center, striking both with the stance and with the inside edge of the wrist into the groin (out breath). This movement will turn farther and angle into the opponent. The entire sequence rotates through almost 360 degrees, and the final entry strike finishes with the defender essentially facing forward again, since the opponent will have been turned somewhat with the arm bar.

5. The entire sequence is now repeated on the other hand, beginning
   with rising fist strikes on the in breath. This time, visualize the attack
   as coming from the front. This attack is answered by raising the body
   and striking with the fists into the wrist tendons, starting with an in
   breath. As an alternate interpretation, if the opponent attacks with a
   bear hug from the rear, the rising fists can take off an the encircling
   arm, lift it clear of the head while turning, and then grip one of the
   arms with both hands, bringing it down in front.

6. Execute the front kick, face, and biceps strikes, breathing out. The rear attacker alternative would continue here with an arm bar, eventually leading into a throw.

7. Cross step, elbow break, adjust the angle if needed (in breath).

8. Enter into the groin strike (breathe out).

9. Turning the head signals a new opponent, whose left punch is trapped and itself struck on the in breath. The captured hand is taken across the body to block the opponent's other hand (detail shown from the other side for clarity).

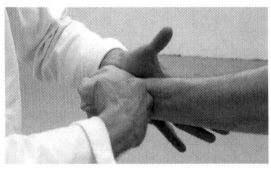

10. The hand is kept trapped, and the arm weakened by striking the biceps with the knuckles from below (out breath).

11. The attacking hand is drawn straight while the opponent is attacked by a front kick on the in breath. This kick can easily be targeted at the opponent's leg instead.

12. Sinking down from the kick, the attacking arm's elbow is struck (breath out).

13. The opponent is struck in the face with the knife hand or fingertips while the arm is slipped and then trapped under the armpit (in breath).

14. The arm is then forced to bend and the elbow lifted with the pullback motion as the other hand attacks the opened lower edge of the rib cage area (out breath).

15. The combination attack continues by crossing away (turning) from the other undamaged hand and applying a second front kick on the in breath.

16. Coming down from the front kick, the captured elbow is shocked again with the left inside blocking motion (out breath). The defender must make distance from the opponent to provide room for the technique.

 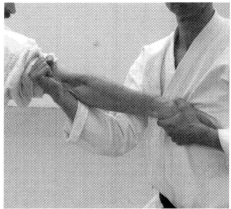

17. As in Tekki Shodan, the arm is pulled upwards on the in breath while attacking the armpit with a punch.

18. Grabbing the shoulder to turn and open the neck area, finish the sequence by executing an inverted rising punch into the carotid artery bifurcation in the neck (out breath: *kiai*).

19. This sequence now repeats on the other hand, beginning with the trap and strike of a new opponent's fist (in breath).

20. Then the biceps strike (out breath). If the attack were visualized as coming with the other hand, the trap and block movement can become a wristlock.

21. Front kick, breathing in while pulling the arm.

22. Elbow break while holding the arm (breathe out). If the distance is too close, alternatives include directly striking into the opponent's torso.

23. Open the target, strike the eyes, and trap the arm (breathe in).

24. Rib cage punch. If the head is taken during the preceding movement, the hook punch can be seen as occurring with a grip on the chin, resulting in a neck break.

25. Cross step and kick (breathe in). A turn also could be visualized here to adjust for either the opponent's position, or alternatively, to shift to a new opponent, as in Tekki Shodan.

26. Elbow break or arm lock (breathe out)

27. Clear the arm away from the target and punch into the armpit (breathe in). If the punch is directed across the opponent's throat, this can become an unbalancing movement or throw itself.

28. Pull the shoulder down and deliver the inverted punch <*kiai*>. If the distance is too close, the grab can be of the head, and the inverted strike can use the elbow instead of the fist as the weapon.

29. This completes the *kata* <*yame*>.

TEKKI SANDAN

The third *kata* in the Tekki series is the most complex in terms of symmetry as well as in terms of the combinations. This *kata* as well has two almost mirror halves, each with two segments, again implying four opponents in the whole *kata*. This *kata* incorporates more joint techniques and more explicit counterattacks on the attacking arm and elbow. The timing is also more varied, and the transitions from opponent to opponent are not as clearly marked. Also, the absolute mirror imaging performance of the left and right halves of the previous *kata* is not seen in this *kata*, making some of the transitions more difficult. While the *kata* can be done with simple alternating breaths for each technique, the breathing used can be changed to a more complicated method, involving at times two focused techniques on not only a single out breath, but also on one in breath, i.e., stepping or segmenting the breath. As a result, there is not a simple formula to determine the breath direction as in the previous *kata*, and breathing directions must be given explicitly. These same directions for this *kata* (and the other 25 *kata* in the JKA curriculum) can be found in the Appendix of the book, *Advanced Karate—Do*.[4] Some of the double in and double out breath techniques can be separated if more power is needed at any particular technique, but at the expense of speed and swift technique linkage. Ultimately, the breathing used will depend on the individual performer's body as well as the opponent's reactions, and should be modified to fit the situation.

1. The initial attack is a combination right handed grab to immobilize the defender's elbow and a left handed punch. The answer is to ignore the grab, parry the left punch with the right hand, and shock the attacking elbow with the inside blocking motion, executed on the in breath.

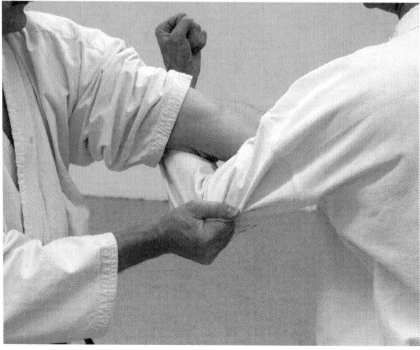

2. The combination continues immediately by circling the blocking hand quickly around the attacking hand to drive it down while striking up into the elbow joint with the right hand, executed on the out breath.

3. Next, cross grab both the opponent's wrists and yank the hand that originally grabbed the defender's elbow across the center line, breathing half in.

4. Pull that hand up and straight while using the left elbow to attack the ribs under the opponent's right nipple on the second half of the in breath while still controlling the original punching hand.

5. Shift the grip of the right hand around the attacker's fist so as to grab that fist from on top. Then thrust the captured fist in an inverted fashion towards the opponent's face, on the first half of the out breath. This produces a twist lock called *sankyo* in aikido. Even if the grip shift should fail, the hand can execute safely an inverted punch to the face by crossing the arm, and can recapture the hand upon its pullback in the next step.

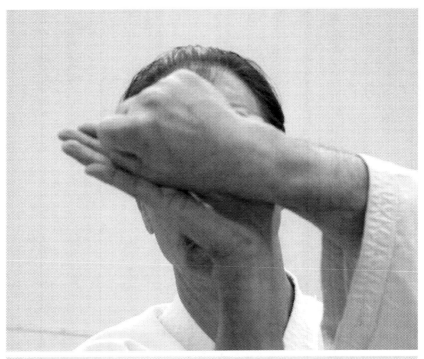

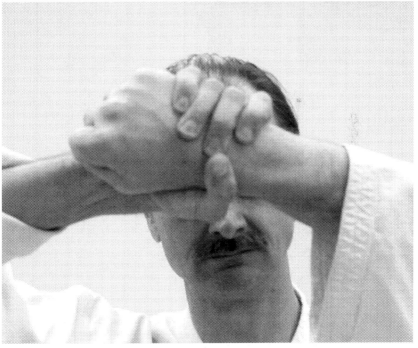

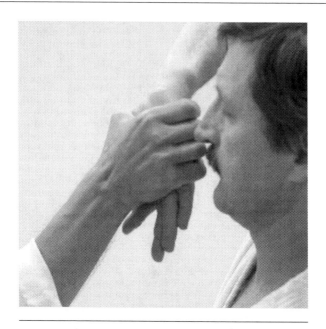

6. Draw the hand back to the hip and, finally releasing the opponent's left hand, trap both hands with pressure just above the elbow of the opponent's right arm, with a small in—breath if possible.

7. Finish the sequence with a punch into the side of the opponent's head with the rest of the out breath.

8. The next movement signals the transition to a new opponent, who has grabbed the previously extended right hand with their own right hand. Trap the grabbing hand during an in breath, and rotate the knuckles into the wrist tendons of the attacker while breathing out to focus the technique. This form resembles the wristlock called *nikyo* in aikido.

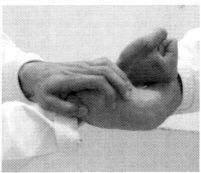

9. Step into and across the opponent, and draw out the attacking arm with the sweeping motion, using a sharp in and out breath. If the defender has the strength, all of this can be done on a single in breath. Adjust the angle as needed during the cross step. Alternatively, simply twist in place, and then shift out.

10. Circle the arm, keeping the opponent's hand trapped so as to set up a shoulder lock, breathing in and then out smoothly. If the previous technique was done in a single in breath, this technique can be done as a single out breath as well to gain speed.

11. Clear the locking hand, but keep the arm trapped on an in breath, and punch into the side of the opponent's head with the subsequent partial out breath. The hand shape in the trap resembles aikido's *sankyo* technique (defender's left hand twisting attacker's right palm).

12. Quickly follow up by using the combined down and inside block movements to force the opponent's elbow into a bend with the point of the elbow upwards on the second half of the same out breath. Alternatively, simply execute a raking strike to the nerves along the inner upper arm with the thumb knuckle.

13. Reverse the motions to attack the elbow joint again, trapping the hand in the crook of the left arm, while starting to breathe in.

14. Pull the opponent's left arm back while punching the face again, completing the in breath.

15. Grab with the right hand, and finish the sequence with another rising inverted punch with an out breath expressed as a *kiai*.

16. The *kata* now begins its second "mirror" half. Begin by stepping across, counter kicking on the in breath, and deflecting an incoming right punch on the out breath, while leaving the left handed grab alone. The "blocking" hand makes a raking back knuckle strike across the opponent's face (out breath). Again, the footwork could be considered a marker for a twisting turn rather than a lateral shift, depending on the attacker's angle.

17. Breathe half in and cross grab the wrists as before.

18. Finish the in breath by yanking the grabbing hand off and pulling the arm out while applying the elbow strike.

19. Breathe out to change grip and apply the driving in wrist twist lock.

20. Breathe slightly in to draw the arm out and trap, and immediately breathe out to punch.

21. Assuming a new opponent, breathe in to trap and breathe out to lock the wrist.

22. Step across (or twist in place), and step to draw out the arm, breathing in.

23. Circle to the shoulder lock, breathing out.

24. Trap, breathing in, and punch, breathing out.

25. The symmetry of the *kata* breaks here in order to allow a return to the starting position at the conclusion, using the same techniques seen in the previous Tekki *kata*. The *bunkai* are the same as before. The trapped arm is cleared to the right, retaining control of the fist, and the opponent straightened up on an in breath.

26. The arm is again trapped, bending the elbow and arching the opponent while the lower rib cage (spleen) is attacked with a hook punch, breathing out. The drawback hand can pull, lift, or grip as indicated by the opponent's reactions.

27. Moving away from the opponent's free arm, make distance with the step across, and kick while breathing in, adjusting the angle as needed.

28. Slide out along the trapped arm, and strike the elbow, breathing out.

29. Breathe half in to use the double "blocking" movement to again attack the elbow joint or inner upper arm nerves with a raking strike.

30. Complete the in breath to grab and pull the arm up while punching into the exposed armpit rib area.

31. Grab the opponent's shoulder and finish the sequence with the inverted punch on an out breath as before *<kiai>*.

32. This completes the *kata <yame>*.

CONCLUDING COMMENTS

The Tekki series of *kata* are relatively straightforward in their interpretation. Once the *bunkai* have been practiced with a partner, there are almost no techniques in them that are either very complex or require extreme exactitude to perform for adequate effect.

The root concepts of the self—defenses presented above include the following points:

1. Damage and then control the incoming limb(s) while avoiding the main attack vector.

2. Keep control of the opponent by using off balancing movements and remaining physically attached.

3. As far as possible, always have both hands engaged with the opponent.

4. Move away from or interdict any remaining threatening limb(s) as the situation evolves.

5. For any technique, have a backup and/or a continuation technique in case the opponent does not submit or the technique fails.

6. Escalate the defense combination with progressive techniques that move inwards towards the opponent's body (head, neck, or torso) and produce increasing amounts of damage. However, be aware that at any time, the combination can stop, provided the opponent submits.

From the point of view of *kata* analysis, at least these other points should become clear, and can be applied to any *kata*:

1. "Label disease" is to be avoided — just because a technique has been named "block" or "punch" for teaching convenience does not mean that this is the movement's sole purpose. On the other hand, at times a punch is just a punch.

2. All portions of a technique's movement including any "setup" and/or compensating "pullback" motions, are probably involved with the opponent and exist to either damage or control that opponent in some manner. The "technique" is not to be found in the static terminal posture, but in the complete dynamic movement leading into that posture. The *kata* trains the terminal posture to insure adequate dynamics, not to demonstrate the actual position attained.

3. The techniques of aikido, jujitsu and/or judo can provide keys to many of the movements in the *kata* that seem forced or implausible if viewed only from a tournament karate perspective.

A final consideration is this: In my opinion, one must view the *kata* as movies — dynamic sequences — rather than as a slide show of stills. Actual techniques are "verbs", and not the "nouns" used to label them. Each *kata* has scenes that are longer than one or two techniques, and the movements form a coherent whole with recurring themes. These themes are the stamp of the originator of the *kata* and provide an insight into this person's approach to self—defense. By practicing a wide range of *kata*, one can be exposed to many such teachers. This will allow one not only to find a "favorite" *kata* that resonates with one's own self, but also become aware of alternative techniques that one might be forced to face.

ENDNOTES

[1] Johnson, N. Zen Shaolin Karate, Tuttle, Rutland, VT, 1994.

[2] Clark, R. Martial Arts for the University, Kendall/Hunt, DuBuque, IA, 1992.

[3] Annesi, A. Cracking The Kata Code — How Does A Kata Mean?, Bushido—Kai, Framingham, MA, 1992.

[4] Schmeisser, E.T. Advanced Karate—Do. Focus Publications., St. Louis, MO, 1994.

.

Printed in the United States
By Bookmasters